JAN 1 4 2010

D1061266

INVENTIONS THAT CHANGED THE WORLD

THE AUTOMOBILE

BY EMILY ROSE OACHS

Clinton Macomb
Public Library

BLASTOFF!
DISCOVERY

Bellwether Media • Minneapolis, MN

Blastoff! Discovery launches
a new mission: reading to learn.
Filled with facts and features, each
book offers you an exciting new
world to explore!

This edition first published in 2019 by Bellwether Media, Inc.

No part of this publication may be reproduced in whole or in
part without written permission of the publisher.
For information regarding permission, write to Bellwether
Media, Inc., Attention: Permissions Department,
6012 Blue Circle Dr., Minnetonka, MN 55343.

Library of Congress Cataloging-in-Publication Data

Names: Oachs, Emily Rose, author.
Title: The Automobile / by Emily Rose Oachs.
Description: Minneapolis, MN : Bellwether Media, Inc.,
   2019. | Series: Blastoff! Discovery. Inventions that Changed
   the World | Includes bibliographical references and index.
   |Audience: Ages 7-13.
Identifiers: LCCN 2018040245 (print) | LCCN 2018041603
   (ebook) | ISBN 9781681037004 (ebook) | ISBN
   9781626179660 (hardcover : alk. paper)
   | ISBN 9781618915092 (pbk. : alk. paper)
Subjects: LCSH: Automobiles–History–Juvenile literature. |
   Transportation, Automotive–History–Juvenile literature.
Classification: LCC TL147 (ebook) | LCC TL147 .O234 2019
   (print) | DDC 629.22209–dc23
LC record available at https://lccn.loc.gov/2018040245

Text copyright © 2019 by Bellwether Media, Inc. BLASTOFF!
DISCOVERY and associated logos are trademarks
and/or registered trademarks of Bellwether Media, Inc.
SCHOLASTIC, CHILDREN'S PRESS, and associated logos are
trademarks and/or registered trademarks of Scholastic Inc.,
557 Broadway, New York, NY 10012.

Editor: Betsy Rathburn   Designer: Josh Brink

Printed in the United States of America, North Mankato, MN

TABLE OF CONTENTS

A CROSS-COUNTRY JOURNEY

Standing in their driveway, a family loads suitcases into the trunk of their car. Then, they climb into the vehicle. Behind them, the garage door closes slowly.

The car pulls out of the driveway as they all wave goodbye to their house. They will see it again in a few weeks. It is time to get on the road!

Many miles pass beneath the tires. Few other automobiles share the highway with the family's car. The family is soon far outside of the city.

Eventually, the sun begins to set. The family stops at a roadside motel. The day might be over, but their trip continues tomorrow. The family's automobile has paved the way to adventure!

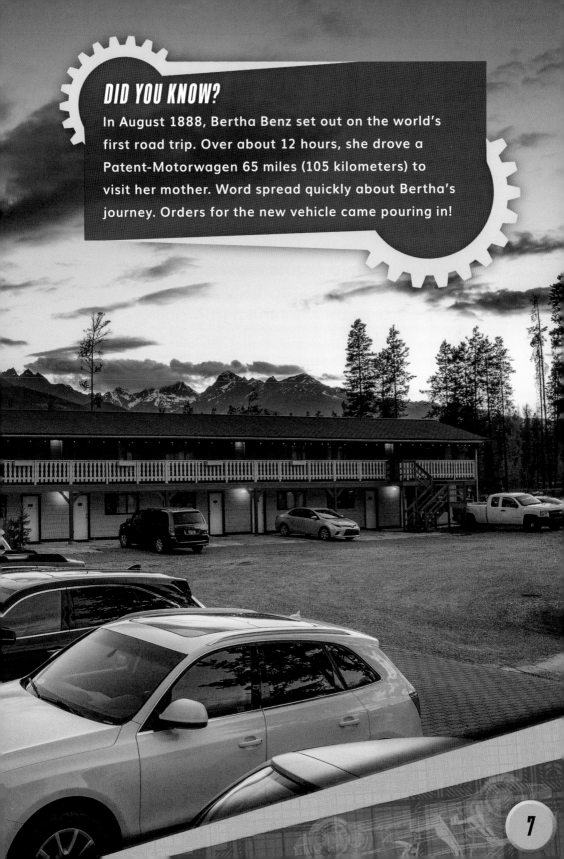

DID YOU KNOW?

In August 1888, Bertha Benz set out on the world's first road trip. Over about 12 hours, she drove a Patent-Motorwagen 65 miles (105 kilometers) to visit her mother. Word spread quickly about Bertha's journey. Orders for the new vehicle came pouring in!

FROM CARRIAGES TO CARS

Designs for self-moving vehicles date as far back as the 1400s. In 1769, an inventor named Nicolas-Joseph Cugnot built a steam-powered tricycle. Many consider it to be the first automobile. By 1830, steam buses transported people through major cities.

Nicolas-Joseph Cugnot's steam-powered tricycle

Étienne Lenoir's internal combustion engine

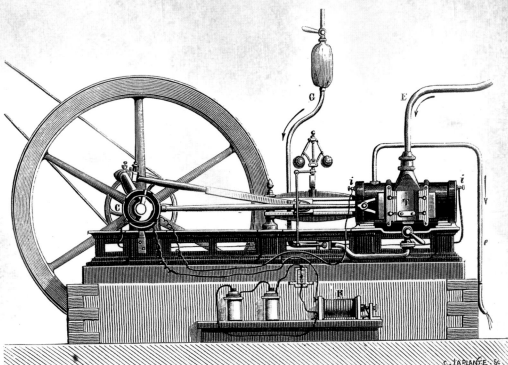

In 1859, Étienne Lenoir introduced the first successful **internal combustion engine**. Though smaller than a steam engine, it could produce the same amount of power. Many inventors improved its design in the following decades. The internal combustion engine became even more **efficient**!

9

KARL BENZ

Born:	November 25, 1844, in Mühlberg, Germany
Background:	Bicycle mechanic who studied mechanical engineering at the University of Karlsruhe
Automobile Invented:	Benz Patent-Motorwagen
Year Invented:	1886
Idea Development:	Karl Benz built many related inventions in the years before he developed the Motorwagen. He patented his designs for spark plugs, throttle systems, and a clutch. He combined these with a four-stroke engine to create the Motorwagen. After a long-distance journey, he decided to add a gear system to the car's design.

In 1876, Nikolaus Otto **patented** the **four-stroke engine**. It used less fuel than previous engines. Karl Benz used one in his three-wheeled Patent-Motorwagen in 1886. The next year, Gottlieb Daimler created the first four-wheeled automobile!

By 1900, the birth of the automobile was complete. Soon, automobiles almost completely replaced the horse-drawn carriages of the past. To **consumers**, cars meant new freedom. Automobiles could take people wherever they wanted to go. They gave people greater control over their lives!

four-stroke engine

INSIDE AUTOMOBILES

As time passed, carmakers experimented with different designs. In 1893, the Duryea brothers created an automobile by attaching an engine to a horse carriage. Instead of a steering wheel, a **tiller** guided the vehicle. This model was the first gas-powered automobile on America's streets!

The 1901 Mercedes 35 HP featured a modern design. The long car sat low to the ground. It was built around the lightweight 35-horsepower engine. A **carburetor** fed fuel into the engine's four **cylinders**. The new **honeycomb radiator** helped cool the engine!

1901 Mercedes 35 HP

FOUR-STROKE ENGINE

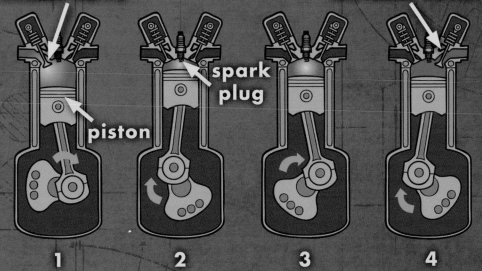

intake valve

exhaust valve

spark plug

piston

1   2   3   4

1. Intake:
Fuel is drawn into the piston from the open intake valve.

2. Compression:
The piston rises and compresses fuel. The intake valve closes, and the spark plug combusts.

3. Combustion:
The piston is forced down by the spark plug's combustion.

4. Exhaust:
The exhaust valve opens, and the piston rises to push exhaust through the valve.

In 1908, the famous Ford Model T began its 19-year run. Foot pedals switched gears. A **throttle** on the steering wheel controlled the car's speed. Like other early automobiles, the Model T used a **hand-crank engine**.

Ford Model T

DID YOU KNOW?

Hand cranks were difficult to use. Drivers had to turn them with a lot of force to start their cars. Calling a person "cranky" comes from how grumpy people grew after turning hand cranks!

**1922 Duesenberg
Model A**

In 1912, Cadillac introduced the **electric starter**. Starting a car's engine became safer and easier. In 1922, the Duesenberg Model A was the first passenger car in America to feature **hydraulic brakes**. These made automobiles safer!

1922 Essex coach

Many familiar car features appeared early on. The 1922 Essex coach was the first car with a hard top. In the 1930s, Nash Motor Company produced the first cars with modern heaters and air conditioners. In 1930, the invention of the car radio meant drivers no longer traveled in silence.

Early carmakers also included equipment to make automobiles safer. In 1939, Buick first offered turn signals on all new cars. Volvo installed the first modern seatbelts in their cars in 1959. Cars with airbags hit the market in 1968.

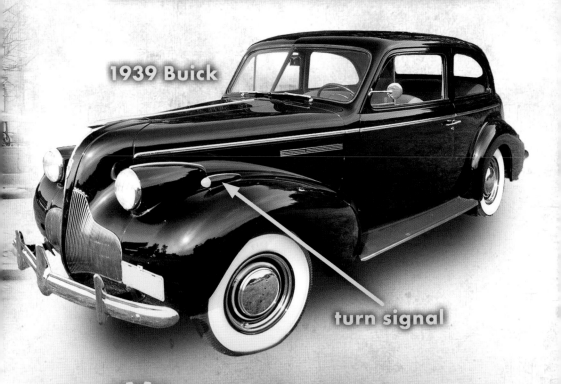

1939 Buick

turn signal

DID YOU KNOW?

The National Highway Traffic Safety Administration believes many people owe their lives to seatbelts. It estimates that seatbelts save 11,000 lives in the United States each year!

navigation system

Starting in the 1970s, carmakers began adding computers to automobiles. This helped make cars more efficient. Later, **navigation** systems were added to help drivers get around. Today, smartphone connections allow drivers to make calls and play music. DVD players entertain passengers on long drives.

Today's cars range from the tiny smart car to the stretch limousine. Many are passenger vehicles. Pickup trucks have open trunks to hold cargo. Sport-utility vehicles let drivers steer off of main roads. Automobiles have changed a lot since they were first invented. But they still get people where they need to go!

limousine

smart car

THE AGE OF THE AUTOMOBILE

The automobile sparked many changes for people around the world. People no longer had to rely on railroads. In the United States, more than 40 million automobiles were on the roads by the 1950s!

DID YOU KNOW?

Over 19 years, Ford Motor Company sold 15 million Model Ts. At one point, assembly lines were finishing as many as 10,000 Model Ts in a single day!

Around that time, many Americans moved to new communities called **suburbs**. Cars helped them travel farther for work. Soon, a long network of highways connected one coast to the other. By 1980, almost nine out of ten American households had at least one car.

Automobiles also changed manufacturing. Early on, teams of workers built one car at a time. But in 1913, Ford began using the **assembly line** for car manufacturing. Assembly lines made building Model Ts quicker and more affordable.

Each assembly line worker was assigned a specific job. The car's body moved through the room. Workers completed their job as the car passed. Assembly lines made it possible to **mass-produce** cars. Today, they are used to build cars, toys, and many other items!

assembly line

FORD MODEL T

Inventor's Name: Henry Ford

Year of Release: 1908

Uses: Henry Ford built the Model T to be an everyday car. He wanted it to be affordable for ordinary people. The car's design allowed it to travel on rough roads. This long-lasting vehicle is one of the best-selling automobiles in history.

Both new and old **industries** boomed as the popularity of cars grew. More jobs were available in oil and steel. Cars boosted the road construction and rubber industries. Gas stations and mechanic shops opened to support motorists. New diners and motels also appeared along roadsides.

Not all of the car's impacts have been positive. Scientists have learned that burning gasoline pollutes the air. In response, more carmakers are working to put electric and **hybrid** cars on the market.

DID YOU KNOW?

The automobile even gave rise to new types of entertainment. NASCAR, IndyCar, and Formula One racing draw millions of fans from around the world. The first American car race took place in 1895!

electric car

A DRIVERLESS FUTURE

The automobile will see many new advances in the future. Among the biggest is the self-driving vehicle. Features like park-assist already shift command from the human driver to the car. Yet new technology may give cars even more control.

car with park-assist

DID YOU KNOW?

Inventors are working to create a flying car. Wings that flip in and out would allow the vehicle to drive on regular city streets or fly through the air!

Some car companies are testing self-driving cars. Experts believe they could actually make roads a safer place. Some think self-driving cars will be widely available as early as 2020. Less than 150 years after Karl Benz completed his first drive, cars may not need a driver at all!

AUTOMOBILE TIMELINE

1769
Nicolas-Joseph Cugnot invents a steam-powered automobile

1893
The Duryea brothers create the earliest successful American gas-powered car

1886
Karl Benz patents the first true gas-powered automobile

1908
The Model T is released

1959
The first vehicle uses modern seatbelts

2008
Tesla releases its first all-electric car, the Roadster

2019-
Future developments

1913
The Ford Motor Company begins using the assembly line

2009
Google begins testing self-driving cars

GLOSSARY

assembly line—a method of production in which workers perform specific tasks on objects as they pass

carburetor—a part in the engine where fuel and air combine

consumers—people who buy goods

cylinders—hollow chambers inside the engine in which fuel burns to move the pistons

efficient—working with little waste

electric starter—a device that uses electricity to start an engine

four-stroke engine—an internal combustion engine that requires a piston to make four strokes to create energy

hand-crank engine—a type of engine started by turning a crank by hand with great force

honeycomb radiator—a device that uses rectangular tubes to spread cooling water through an engine

hybrid—a car with a gas engine and an electric motor

hydraulic brakes—brakes that release a fluid when the pedal is pressed

industries—types of businesses that make a particular good or perform a specific service

internal combustion engine—a type of engine with cylinders in which fuel burns

mass-produce—to build many at a time

navigation—the process of determining one's position and creating a route

patented—protected with a document that gives an inventor all rights to create and sell their invention

suburbs—small communities at the edge of a city

throttle—the lever that controls how much fuel an engine receives

tiller—a handle that a driver turns to steer a vehicle from side to side

TO LEARN MORE

AT THE LIBRARY

Bailey, Diane. *How the Automobile Changed History*.
Minneapolis, Minn.: Abdo Publishing, 2016.

Mara, Wil. *Henry Ford: Automotive Innovator*. New York, N.Y.:
Children's Press, 2018.

Vilardi, Debbie. *Electric Cars*. Minneapolis, Minn.: Pop, 2018.

ON THE WEB

FACTSURFER

Factsurfer.com gives you
a safe, fun way to find
more information.

1. Go to www.factsurfer.com.

2. Enter "automobile" into the search box.

3. Click the "Surf" button and select your
   book cover to see a list of related web sites.

INDEX

The images in this book are reproduced through the courtesy of: Steve Lagreca, front cover (center); Stanislaw Tokarski, front cover (bottom), p. 28 (Model T); Creativa Images, p. 4; tomas devera photo, p. 5; miroslav_1, pp. 6-7; Print Collector/ Getty Images, p. 8; World History Archive/ Alamy, p. 9; Wikipedia, p. 10 (left); A.Sontaya, p. 10 (right); Science & Society Picture Library/ Getty Images, p. 11; Mark W Lucey, pp. 12, 28 (gas-powered car); J HIME, p. 14; Rex Gray/ Wikipedia, p. 15; Everett Collection Historical/ Alamy, p. 16; Greg Gjerdingen/ Wikipedia, p. 17; otherstock, p. 18; Art Konovalov, p. 19 (all); H. Armstrong Roberts/ Stringer/ Getty Images, pp. 20-21; Hulton Archive/ Stringer/ Getty Images, p. 22; LagunaticPhoto, p. 23; Aladdin Color Inc/ Getty Images, p. 24; d13, p. 25; Flystock, p. 26; VanderWolf Images, p. 27 (inset); Mastroraf, p. 28 (steam-powered automobile); KS-Art, p. 28 (gas-powered automobile); Wikimedia Commons, p. 29 (assembly line); Mega Pixel, p. 29 (seatbelt); Frontpage, p. 29 (Tesla); jessicakirshcreative, p. 29 (self-driving car); Kobby Dagan, p. 29 (future car).